ROSE

BOOK FOUR

Written and Illustrated by

M. Khalilah Muhammad, Ph.D.

Order this book online at www.trafford.com
or email orders@trafford.com

Most Trafford titles are also available at major online book retailers.

 www.trafford.com

North America & international
toll-free: 844 688 6899 (USA & Canada)
fax: 812 355 4082

Our mission is to efficiently provide the world's finest, most comprehensive book publishing
service, enabling every author to experience success. To find out how to publish your book,
your way, and have it available worldwide, visit us online at www.trafford.com

Because of the dynamic nature of the Internet, any web addresses or links contained in
this book may have changed since publication and may no longer be valid. The views
expressed in this work are solely those of the author and do not necessarily reflect the views
of the publisher, and the publisher hereby disclaims any responsibility for them.

ISBN: 978-1-6987-1368-7 (sc)
ISBN: 978-1-6987-1367-0 (e)

Library of Congress Control Number: 2022923275

Print information available on the last page.

Trafford rev. 12/13/20222

For my Beautiful Children:

Ashanti, Jameel, Nadirah, Najlah, and Zafir
Without whom I would never have been
able to slow down enough to smell the Roses
And

Reflect on My Life.

ABOUT THE AUTHOR

Born to an ex-military and retired Firefighter and an Educator, Dr. M. Khalilah Muhammad was always reading and examining books and developing her writing skills and the skill of open expression. Due to her father's military background, Dr. Muhammad traveled extensively. She loves visiting new places and experiencing new horizons.

As a child, Dr. Muhammad would spend time in the yard playing with worms and examining the gardens her parents established. There were floral gardens and vegetable gardens in her yard. She would assist in the upkeep of the gardens and the yard.

After a hard day's work, Dr. Muhammad, would sit on the porch and marvel at the bounties of life. One of her favorite relaxation tools is gardening. The second favorite was taking time to enjoy the beach, waves, and life at rest and reflection.

Dr. Muhammad is an epidemiologist. She studies trends of disease and loves traveling and exploring the world. She was told once by a childhood friend to make sure to, "take time and smell the roses". In doing so, she wanted to spend time in the environment and marvel at creation! Dr. Muhammad currently resides in Georgia.

How does a rose bloom?

What does a rose need to bloom?

The rose needs fertilizer, pruning, water and sunshine.

When you look into the rose, there is a softness on the inside petals.

The rose petals last up to 3 days when they are taken off of the flower. They last up to one week when you have them in a cool place with flower food in a vase.

You must change the water in the vase one time every two to three days and make sure to take all of the leaves and flowers that fall into the water out when you refresh the rose water.

Roses on the bush need to be in at least four hours of direct sunlight to thrive.

Roses bloom in the spring.

Prune the rose bush in the winter. The winter and frost will slow down the growth of the rose bushes.

When it is hot outside, the growth of the rose bush is sped up.

There are bloom cycles for roses that start in the winter. This is when you deadhead the rose bush and feed the bush an organic fertilizer.

Watch the rose bush foliage...cut and remove the stems that are not going to make the bush look right when it blooms. This is when the stems are around two inches long and you are using nitrogen in the soil. You want them to be straight up and not blocking any walkways. You can get nitrogen from the coffee grounds that you shake at the base of the rose bush.

The third cycle is the blooming period when you see rose buds and you slow down on using nitrogen and start using phosphorus.

Phosphorus will make the blooms larger. Now you can have disbudding where you cut off small side buds from the stem if you want a single bloom.

If you want a lot of roses that are called a spray, you do not need to disbud. Side buds will also grow side buds too!

In the fourth cycle, the rose stem is long. The buds are large. The roses are almost ready.

The sepals have not opened. Stop using the nitrogen now. Use iron supplementation. This will make the rose foliage dark.

The last phase is the period when the roses bloom.

The roses do not need to be fed. Make sure during this stage to clear all growth that is in the way. Try to keep the rose blooms protected from the water because water that stays on the blooms will leave spots on the petals.

What can you use to get phosphorus in the rose garden?

Banana Peels!!! Chop up some banana peels and bury them under the leaves of the rose. Make sure that they are away from the stem. You can also use a blender to blend up the banana peels with water like a compost then pour it on the dirt around the rose bush.

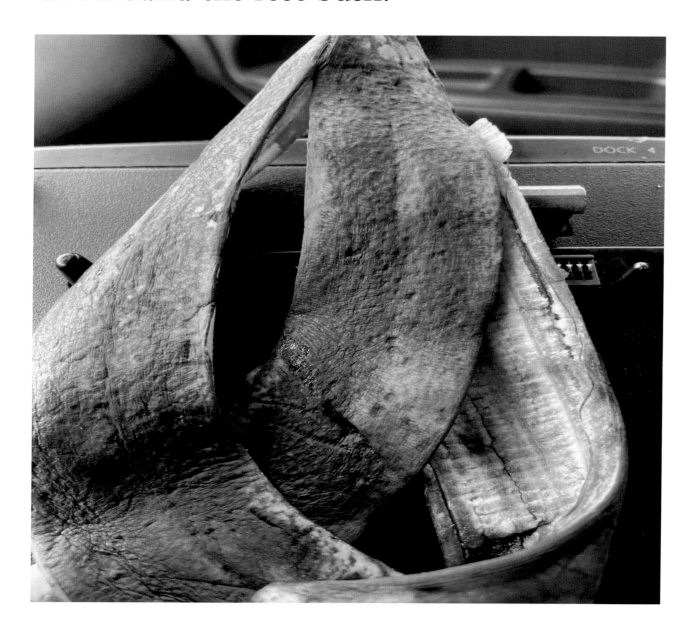

Make sure to prune the roses throughout the year and each season.

You can also keep the egg shells from breakfast! Crush them and shake them on the dirt around the rose bush so that the calcium from the shells will benefit the bush.

You MUST take care of a rose, be loyal to it and give attention to the needs of the rose in order for the rose to bloom beautifully and come back each year.

WORD FIND

There are 19 words in this puzzle. Parents, you may copy this page for your child and make it into a game! See who can finish first. Have fun!

```
P Q B E S R O Q B A N A N A D
H E E F I E R D U I G L B H E
O R T B S A G E D E R F U Q A
S K B A X K A H N H C D G F D
P E E L L G N V G O N P S E H
H Y V U M H I R M O E B E R E
O F O M D X C P G Z G W G T A
R W O Q C S O O H V O F A I D
U G S W S S L O Z W R S I L M
S E N D T P O L L E T T L I R
O W O P L M R O S E I O O Z A
L E R A D O I A M T N O F E F
T R I N R O U O Y B F H L R S
C Y C L E L S O I L M U Y I G
W I D I S B U D J R A W Q N X
```

WORDS FOUND

So, how many words did you find???
List them below.

1. _____

2. _____

3. _____

4. _____

5. _____

6. _____

7. _____

8. _____

9. _____

10. _____

11. _____

12. _____

13. _____

14. _____

15. _____

16. _____

17. _____

18. _____

19. _____

GREAT JOB!!

Hmmm.....Did you find the following?

Phosphorus

Peel

Petal

Organic

Bud

Banana

Deadhead

Fertilizer

Foliage

Stem

Rose

Nitrogen

Compost

Spray

Soil

Cycle

Bloom

Iron

GREAT JOB!

Thank You For your Support!